The Terrible Power of House Rabbit

SUSAN GATES

Illustrated by Martin Remphry

OXFORD
UNIVERSITY PRESS

OXFORD
UNIVERSITY PRESS

Great Clarendon Street, Oxford OX2 6DP

Oxford University Press is a department of the University of Oxford.
It furthers the University's objective of excellence in research, scholarship,
and education by publishing worldwide in

Oxford   New York

Auckland   Cape Town   Dar es Salaam
Hong Kong   Karachi   Kuala Lumpur   Madrid
Melbourne   Mexico City   Nairobi   New Delhi
Shanghai   Taipei   Toronto

With Offices in

Argentina   Austria   Brazil   Chile   Czech Republic
France   Greece   Guatemala   Hungary   Italy   Japan
South Korea   Poland   Portugal   Singapore   Switzerland
Thailand   Turkey   Ukraine   Vietnam

Oxford is a registered trade mark of Oxford University Press
in the UK and in certain other countries

First published 1999

10 9 8 7 6 5

ISBN-13: 978 0 19 9187140
ISBN-10: 0 19 9187142

Printed in Great Britain

Illustrations by Martin Remphry
Photograph of Susan Gates by Pauline Holbrook

CHAPTER 1

Keep your mouth shut, Ben!

I *knew* there was something sinister about that rabbit from the very first time I saw him.

Dad bought him for Toby, my little brother.

Toby loves rabbits. But he can't keep a rabbit in a hutch. He's got asthma. The straw and sawdust make him wheeze and cough.

One day Dad said, 'Toby, would you like a House Rabbit?'

Toby said, 'What kind of rabbit is that?'

'A new kind of rabbit. You don't need a hutch. It lives in your house like a cat or a dog.'

'It sounds like the perfect rabbit for Toby,' said Mum.

Mum wouldn't have said that if she'd known what was going to happen.

Dad brought House Rabbit home. He was a very smart-looking rabbit. He was big, and black and white. His coat was glossy and sleek as a penguin's.

But, as I said before, there was something sinister about him. I noticed it straight away.

It was his eyes. They were pink and goggly. And when he stared at you – well, you felt really uncomfortable.

You squirmed about, as if a teacher was telling you off.

But Toby was delighted with him. He said, 'I love my new pet. I've thought of a name for him. It's Fluffy.'

Fluffy! I thought. *I can't call him that!* He didn't look like a Fluffy to me. Fluffies are soft and cuddly. They don't have cold, sparkling eyes like he had.

But Mum and Dad were really pleased that Toby was pleased. So I warned myself, *Keep your mouth shut, Ben.*

Mum put down a cat litter tray.

'House Rabbits are trained to use this,' she said.

We all watched to see if he was trained.

He did a pile of rabbit droppings in the cat litter tray. It was a very neat pile, like a tiny pyramid.

Mum was thrilled. 'What a clever rabbit!' she said. 'Look how tidy and clean he is!'

'He won't like it here then,' laughed Dad, 'if he's a tidy rabbit. We're the world's untidiest family, aren't we, Ben?'

Dad was right. We should be in the *Guinness Book of Records*.

'We're far too messy for him!' Dad grinned.

Dad thought he was being funny. But House Rabbit didn't see the joke. He stared at Dad. And his eyes were as frosty as pink ice.

CHAPTER 2

I'm in the wrong house

I always get home from school first, before Mum and Toby. I let myself in with my own key.

Next day, as soon as I opened the door, I called, 'House Rabbit.'

I thought, *He'll be pleased to see me. He's been on his own all day.*

I threw my coat on the floor, just like I always do.

Like magic, House Rabbit appeared.

'Hello, House Rabbit! What've you been doing all day?'

He looked squeaky clean. His black and white coat was penguin sleek. There wasn't a hair out of place.

I smoothed down my own hair. Some grass and a dead beetle fell out. And I don't know why, but I felt that I had to apologize.

'Sorry, I've been playing football,' I explained to House Rabbit. 'I don't always look this messy.'

House Rabbit stared at me ... as if to say, *Oh yes?* Then he stared at my coat. He didn't blink once. Then he looked at me again.

And I knew. Don't ask me how. I just knew what he wanted.

'Come on – I never hang my coat up! Not ever!'

House Rabbit wasn't impressed. He just carried on, staring at my coat ...

I laughed, sort of nervously. I thought, *He's only a rabbit! I'm not going to be bossed about by a rabbit!*

But he flashed me one look from those menacing eyes and, somehow, I couldn't resist.

'All right, House Rabbit,' I heard myself saying. 'I've got the message. You win. I'll tidy it up.'

And I could hardly believe it myself. I hung my coat on the peg!

I went into the living room. I thought, *I'm in the wrong house!*

It was spooky. It was as bare as a moon crater.

There were no toys anywhere. No sign that children lived here at all.

'Where's my castle gone? I was in the middle of building it! I was building it for Toby!'

House Rabbit wrinkled his nose. It seemed to be pointing into the corner. Then I saw my castle.

It was in little bits, back in the box of Lego bricks.

'Who did that? Who tidied my castle away?'

Mum wouldn't do that. If she sees we've got an important project – like building a castle – she leaves our things where they are.

House Rabbit's pink eyes glittered.

'And someone's tidied my book away!' I roared. 'What's going on? I left it open on that chair. I've lost my page now!'

House Rabbit just stared at me. He was as calm as custard.

An alarming, unbelievable thought
pinged into my brain. 'Wait a minute!'
I said to House Rabbit. 'Did you do this?
What've you been doing all day? You
haven't been cleaning and tidying up,
by any chance, have you?'

Of course, House Rabbit didn't
answer.

'You're going crazy!' I told myself.
'You're talking to a rabbit. You're
actually asking it if it's been tidying up!'

But then a look crept over House Rabbit's face. It was a smug, self-satisfied look. His pink eyes swept sternly round the room, as if to say, *That's better, isn't it?*

Then he flicked his tail like a feather duster over my shoes. He was giving them a good polish now!

'Stop cleaning my shoes!' I roared at him. 'At least wait until I've taken them off! Listen to me! I hate it when people tidy my things away! Especially when I'm in the middle of doing something important!'

When Mum and Toby came home, I said, 'Someone's tidied my things away! Things that I needed! You didn't tidy them away, did you, Mum?'

Mum looked puzzled. 'Of course I didn't. How could I? I've been out at work all day.'

'It was House Rabbit then! I couldn't believe it at first. But it must have been him! He's spent the whole day tidying and cleaning!'

Mum shook her head and raised her eyebrows: 'Ben, you do say the weirdest things!' She thought I was just being silly.

But Toby was angry with me. 'Why won't you call my rabbit Fluffy?' he said. 'His name is Fluffy!'

But I just couldn't. How can you call a rabbit Fluffy when he's got eyes like a killer shark?

'Come here, Fluffy,' said Toby.

House Rabbit lolloped over. Toby threw his arms around him and gave him a great big hug, as if he was as cute and cuddly as a kitten!

Toby glared at me. 'And don't call my Fluffy stupid,' he said. 'He lives here too. This is his house too. And he doesn't like things lying around. He's a very tidy rabbit. Even his rabbit droppings are tidy.'

'For goodness' sake!' I yelled. 'I'm not tidying up for a rabbit. I like things the way they are!'

'Yes you are, Ben,' said Toby. 'We've all got to. If it'll make my Fluffy happy.'

'Mum?' I looked at Mum desperately. 'Tell him he's talking rubbish.'

But Mum wouldn't. Even she had fallen under House Rabbit's spell!

She shrugged and said, 'Well, I suppose it wouldn't hurt if we were a bit more tidy.'

'What's happening to everyone?'
I wailed. 'I don't like the house like this!
I know where everything is when it's
messy. I can't find anything when it's
tidy!'

But no one was listening to me. They
were making a big fuss of House Rabbit.

He seemed very pleased with himself.
His eyes were glowing like red search-
lights. And he was looking at me, as if
to say, 'I'm the boss here. This is my
house now. And things are going to
change!'

CHAPTER 3

Has everyone gone bananas?

Those searchlight eyes were everywhere.
Every time I turned round, House Rabbit
was there – checking up on me.

Nowhere was safe. Not even the
bathroom!

Next morning, I left the top off the
toothpaste. I always do that. And I
didn't put my toothbrush back in the
toothbrush holder.

But House Rabbit was there, in the
doorway, giving me that accusing look.

I should have said, 'Go away, Rabbit, you neatness freak. Mind your own business.' I *almost* did!

But House Rabbit shot me another look. And though I thought, *I'm not scared of a rabbit,* there was something about those menacing eyes.

When you looked deep into them, you could almost see red flames dancing! They seemed to control your mind. I had to obey.

I screwed the top back on the toothpaste. I put my toothbrush away. I put the toilet seat back down!
I thought, *What's happening to me?*

House Rabbit twitched his nose, as if to say, 'That's an improvement!' Then he lolloped down the stairs.

I even folded up my pyjamas.

All right, I know *you* probably wouldn't have done it.

But you didn't have House Rabbit following you – checking up on you all the time, giving you those looks …

I thought, *I bet Dad doesn't tidy up. He won't let House Rabbit boss him around.*

I ought to tell you about my dad. He gets crazes. And when he gets a craze, he fills the house with it. He went crazy over mountain-biking. And the house was full of bits of bike.

Now he's crazy over computers. He's buying a new one. And the house is full of computer magazines.

I thought, *Dad won't tidy away his crazes!* Even Mum couldn't get him to be tidy. She tried but she'd given up. She said, 'It's hopeless!' So, if he wouldn't listen to Mum, there was no way, absolutely no way, that Dad would tidy up for a rabbit!

When I went downstairs, Toby and Mum were tidying. But then I got the biggest shock of my life.

Dad came crawling out from behind
the sofa. He had a computer magazine
in his hand.

'I'm just putting these into a nice,
tidy stack,' he explained to me. 'That'll
be a big improvement, won't it?'

Oh, no! I thought, hopelessly. Even
Dad had caught the dreaded tidiness
disease!

He crawled about, picking up more computer magazines. Mum was putting my pens away. They looked like robots who'd been programmed to do nothing else but tidy, tidy, tidy.

'Hey,' I said. 'I need those pens for my homework!'

Toby was picking crumbs off the carpet.

I cried out, 'What's going on?'

I felt as if I'd landed on an alien planet!

Mum turned to look at me. She looked worn-out. She didn't seem happy at all.

She said, 'Toby says we all have to tidy up. He says we mustn't leave the house in a mess. He says Fluffy doesn't like it.'

Dad muttered something. It sounded like, 'For goodness' sake!' But he carried on picking up computer magazines.

I shouted, 'Has everyone gone completely bananas?' Then I felt something burning in to my back. I turned round.

There was House Rabbit in the doorway.

His eyes were blazing like volcanoes. And they were staring straight at me.

I looked deep into those eyes – I just couldn't resist.

There were some toy knights on the table. I'd left them there. They were in the middle of fighting a really exciting battle. But I suddenly thought, *That doesn't look very tidy!*

And, before I could stop myself, I'd scooped them all up. And I lined them up in nice straight lines in a cupboard.

That's an improvement! I thought, as I closed the cupboard door.

CHAPTER 4

This is war!

I couldn't stand it any more. I had to tell someone about House Rabbit and how he'd turned my whole family into tidiness freaks.

I sit next to Melissa at school. She's been my best friend since toddler group. So I tried to explain it to her.

'I liked my house messy,' I told her. 'I hate it now! It's not friendly! It smells of disinfectant!'

'And did you say,' Melissa asked, 'that House Rabbit tidies things away?'

'That's right! He's a neatness fanatic! He spends all day tidying up. And now Mum and Dad and Toby are doing it.

'I've even folded up my pyjamas. Can you believe that? It's as if he's cast an evil spell over us all.'

I thought about House Rabbit, all alone in our house. I thought, *I wonder what he's doing now?*

'Rabbits don't tidy up,' said Melissa.

'House Rabbits do.'

'You're just being silly!'

'I'm not! I'm not! Come to my house, on your way home from school. And then you can see for yourself!'

'All right,' Melissa said. 'I will.'

After school, we crept down our garden path. 'Shhh!' I told Melissa. 'We'll surprise him. We'll sneak round the back and look through the windows.'

We peeped through the windows.

'I can't see a rabbit,' said Melissa. 'Are you sure you're not making this up?'

The carpet was as empty as a desert. There wasn't a single brick or book or magazine anywhere.

'He's here all right,' I said, grimly. 'He's probably upstairs.'

We crept into the kitchen.

'Yow!' I nearly crashed on to the kitchen tiles. 'That pesky rabbit! He's been polishing the floor again!'

'Where is he?' asked Melissa.

'Shhh! I'll go and find him.' I crept upstairs and pushed open my bedroom door.

I knew straight away that something was wrong. It didn't feel like my bedroom any more. It didn't even smell like my bedroom. It smelled of disinfectant.

'Oh no!' I yelled. I didn't want to believe it!

But House Rabbit was just coming out from under my bed. He stared at me, as if to say, *That's better! It's nice and tidy now!*

I was outraged! This time he'd gone too far! 'How dare you!' I yelled at him. 'You're not allowed under my bed! Even Mum doesn't go under there!'

It's my private place, where I keep all my secrets. All the things I need.

I looked underneath. There was just a big empty space. There was nothing left. Not even a speck of dust.

'Where's my book of *One Thousand Jokes*? Where are my vampire teeth? Where's my favourite bit of blanket?'

Everything had gone. My whole collection of precious, personal things.

'What have you done with my things?' I felt really sick inside.

Then I saw what he'd done. He'd put all my precious things in my wastepaper basket. Just as if they were rubbish!

'Those things aren't rubbish! They're things I need!' I yelled, snatching my bit of blanket out.

It was the last straw. You've got to
have one little space. Just one little
space that nobody tidies up!

I was hopping mad.

'This is war!' I told House Rabbit. 'It's
either you or me. This house isn't big
enough for the both of us!'

House Rabbit stayed as calm as
custard. He never seemed to get ruffled.
He stared at me with those raspberry ice-
pop eyes. He didn't blink once. I felt
myself going dizzy – and I dropped to
my knees.

I started crawling about, with my nose just above the carpet!

'Hummm, I spy a biscuit crumb!' I told Melissa as she came into my bedroom. 'I must tidy my bedroom! I must pick this up immediately!'

I was just about to pick it up when Melissa saved me.

She grabbed my arm. 'Come on!' she said. She dragged me downstairs. She didn't stop until we reached the garden.

'Phew,' she said. 'I see what you mean – about the terrible power of House Rabbit.'

I shook my head. I still felt dizzy.

'That's what I was trying to tell you!' I said. 'House Rabbit does that to people. He turns them into tidiness freaks, just like him! He brainwashes them so they've got tidiness on the brain.'

'That's really awful!' said Melissa.

'But how can we stop him? How can we rescue Toby and Mum and Dad? What can we do to make my house friendly again? Like it used to be, before House Rabbit came and spoiled it!'

CHAPTER 5

I can't stand much more

We stood in the garden, thinking hard.

I looked over the field behind our house, to the wood where the wild rabbits lived.

I said, 'Why can't he live in a hutch? Or in a burrow like the wild rabbits do? Why did he have to move in with us?'

'I feel a bit sorry for House Rabbit, actually,' said Melissa.

'What?' I was really shocked.

'How can you feel sorry for him? Even a bit? He's bossy. He's fussy. He's really boring. All he thinks about is tidying!'

'That's the trouble,' said Melissa. 'He needs something else to think about. Something to take his mind off tidying.'

'You mean, like a craze or something?'

'Yes.'

'What kind of crazes do rabbits have?'

I thought of all my dad's crazes – a whole string of them. Mountain-biking? That was no good. Unless you could get rabbit-sized mountain bikes, helmets and cycling shorts.

No, no, that's silly, I told myself. Rabbits can't wear cycling helmets. Where would they put their ears? Think of something sensible!

Then, *ping!* I had a really sensible brain wave.

'What about gardening?' I said. 'My dad had a craze on gardening once. You know, growing flowers and vegetables …'

'Well, it's worth a try,' said Melissa. 'At least it will get him out of the house.'

I went to the back door. 'House Rabbit!' I shouted. 'I've got something to show you!'

He came lolloping up.

I showed him the way out to our garden. It was only a small patch. But it was an excellent garden.

It was a wild garden, with long grass and secret dens and places to hide and play.

House Rabbit stared at our garden. His
nose twitched. His pink eyes glittered.
He seemed very keen to get started.

'Grow some flowers!' I told him. 'Get
gardening! Off you go!'

House Rabbit lolloped off into the
long grass.

'I think it's working!' I whispered to
Melissa.

Melissa went back to her house. Mum and Toby and Dad came home.

We didn't see House Rabbit for hours and hours. Even Toby forgot about him. We were sitting on the floor building a Lego castle and eating crisps. We were having a good time.

Suddenly, I heard scratching at the back door.

'Fluffy!' cried Toby. He leapt up. Our castle fell to pieces.

'Oh no, there are bricks all over the place!' he said. 'I'd better start tidying up! Look at these crumbs! Fluffy won't like that at all!'

I went into the kitchen and opened the back door.

House Rabbit was on the step, gazing at me with his cool pink stare.

'You've been gardening a very long time,' I said to him.

He lolloped in, as if he owned the place.

He picked a blade of grass off his shiny coat. He brushed his muddy footprints off the floor with his tail.

Then he stared at me again, as if to say, *That's nice and tidy now.*

Suddenly, I felt sick and shivery inside. 'Wait a minute!' I asked him. 'What exactly have you been doing out there in the garden?'

I peered out of the back door. The garden looked strange – so cold and blue in the moonlight. I wondered what was wrong with it.

It looked as bleak and as unfriendly as the North Pole.

Then I understood. House Rabbit had tidied up the garden.

He'd nibbled the grass short so that every blade was the same height. He'd chewed the bushes and flowers into tidy stumps. There were no secret dens any more. No mysterious tangly places. Nowhere to play!

'You've spoiled it!' I roared at him. I was really angry. 'It doesn't look like my garden any more!'

But House Rabbit wasn't sorry at all.

He did a neat little pile of rabbit droppings in his cat litter tray. Then he lolloped off to inspect the house, to make sure we'd been keeping it tidy.

I stood on my own in the kitchen. I felt really desperate. I thought, 'I can't stand much more of this. I've got to do something – before he tidies us all to death!'

CHAPTER 6

What will I tell Toby?

'So gardening didn't work then?' asked Melissa at school.

'Huh!' I said. 'No, it didn't! It made things worse! Now we've got a garden that's as tidy as our house!'

'Oh dear,' said Melissa.

I looked at my watch. It was eleven o'clock. I thought about House Rabbit all alone in our house.

'I wonder what he's tidying now?' I said.

'But there's nothing left to tidy, is there?'

'He'll find something,' I told her, gloomily.

Melissa came home with me after school – just to see what House Rabbit had been up to. I opened the back door.

'Watch out for the slippery floor,' I warned Melissa.

But the floor wasn't slippery. It wasn't shiny at all. There was even a cornflake on it that had been there since breakfast! Why hadn't House Rabbit tidied it away?

What's going on? I thought. *Where is he?* We went into the living room.

He was on the sofa, staring out of the window. His eyes weren't cold and menacing any more. They were soft and dreamy. His ears weren't sticking up straight. They were flopped over, all droopy.

I looked out over the fields to where he was looking. But I couldn't see anything. Only the wood.

'What are you looking at, House Rabbit?' I asked.

He didn't seem to hear me. I dropped three Lego bricks on the carpet, *plop, plop, plop*. He didn't care. He didn't even turn his head. His mind wasn't on tidying up at all. He gave a big sigh.

'There's something seriously wrong with him,' I told Melissa. 'He doesn't care about tidying. He must be feeling ill!'

'Wait a minute,' said Melissa. 'I can see what he's staring at.'

'What?'

'Look! There – on the edge of the wood.'

Then I saw it. A little brown rabbit. A wild rabbit.

And its eyes were fixed on our
window. It was staring at House Rabbit.
He was staring back.

'Ahhhh,' said Melissa. 'How sweet! House Rabbit's found a little friend.'

Suddenly, a warm breeze blew through the house. It smelled of grass and green trees. House Rabbit wrinkled his nose. He sniffed it.

'You've left the back door open!' I shouted to Melissa.

But House Rabbit was too quick for us. He leapt off the sofa. He ran out the back door, down the garden path and through the open gate.

'He's escaping!' I yelled.

I was going to dash after him.

But Melissa caught my arm and said,
'Let him go.'

We watched House Rabbit run across
the garden and out in to the fields. The
wild rabbit ran to meet him. They
touched noses. Then they ran together
towards the wood.

On the edge of the wood, House
Rabbit turned round. He took a last look
back at me. I saw his eyes sparkle like
two pink stars. Then he vanished into
the trees with his new friend.

'Oh no!' I cried out. 'What am I going
to tell Toby?'

CHAPTER 7

We're free!

It wasn't as bad as I thought. Toby was upset when I told him. He even cried a little bit.

We all went out searching for House Rabbit in the wood. We all called out for him.

'Fluffy!'

'House Rabbit!'

We looked for neat piles of rabbit droppings. But we didn't call very loud. And we didn't look very hard.

Mum said, 'Don't cry, Toby. I'll get you another House Rabbit.'

Toby stopped crying straight away. 'Err, don't bother, Mum. It's OK.'

Even Toby was pleased that he'd gone.

Our house was friendly again. I finished my castle – at last! My dad got a new craze. It was making kites. There were bits of stick and string all over the kitchen table.

We didn't completely forget about House Rabbit.

Sometimes we wondered what he was doing in the wood.

'I bet those wild rabbits have got the tidiest burrows in the world!' I said.

One day in summer, Melissa and Toby and I were kite flying in the fields behind our house.

Melissa said, 'Look over there! Isn't that House Rabbit?'

He was on the edge of the wood in a bright patch of sunlight. And he wasn't alone.

The little brown rabbit we'd seen from our window was with him. And so were some tiny baby rabbits. Six of them!

They were white and black and brown. They were leaping and playing in the sun all around him.

'House Rabbit has a family of his own!' I cried.

He didn't look as sleek as before. He seemed rather rumpled. In fact, he looked downright untidy. There were even twigs in his coat! But I thought he looked much happier.

'Fluffy!' called Toby. But House Rabbit didn't come any nearer.

'He wants to stay in the wood with the wild rabbits,' said Melissa. 'He belongs with them now.'

'Phew!' I thought. 'Thank goodness.'

'Fluffy!' called Toby again, as if he half-wanted him to come back.

But House Rabbit didn't come back. His pink eyes sparkled once. Then he and his family turned round and they vanished into the trees.

So we're free! House Rabbit has gone for good.

But a strange thing keeps happening.

Every afternoon, when I come home from school, I let myself in the back door. I pull off my coat and I'm just about to drop it in a heap on the floor, when something stops me.

I look over my shoulder. Then I hang the coat neatly on a peg.

Just as if House Rabbit is still there, watching me.

About the author

I know someone called Richard Grantham who loves rabbits. But he couldn't keep them because he was allergic to the straw in their cages. Then one day, he told me, 'I might get a House Rabbit!'

He said, 'They're house-trained and you can take them for walks like a dog.' I said, 'You're joking!' But since then I've discovered they're very popular. Probably not if they're tidiness freaks, though, like the House Rabbit in this story.

Other Treetops books at this level include:
Trapped! by Malachy Doyle
Air Raid! by Jean May
The Booming Boots of Joey Jones by David Clayton
Never Wash Your Hair by Margaret McAllister
A Dog for a Day by Wendy Douthwaite

Also available in packs
Stage 14 pack D	0 19 918716 9
Stage 14 class pack D	0 19 918717 7